OCR

GCSE

Business Studies

Workbook

Business Activity, Marketing and People

Charlene Manton

Contents

1 Business Activity 5
    1.1 The role of business enterprise and entrepreneurship 5
    1.2 Business Planning 10
    1.3 Business Ownership 12
    1.4 Business aims and objectives 19
    1.5 Stakeholders in business 19
    1.6 Business growth 23

2 Marketing 36
    2.1 The role of marketing 36
    2.2 Market research 37
    2.3 Market Segmentation 45
    2.4 The marketing mix 50

3 People 54
    3.1 The role of human resources 66
    3.2 Organisational structures and different ways of working 66
    3.3 Communication in business 69
    3.4 Recruitment and selection 76
    3.5 Motivation and retention 81
    3.6 Training and development 85
    3.7 Employment law 90

1 Business Activity

1.1 The role of business enterprise and entrepreneurship

Define the key words

Goods

Services

Profit

Tangible

Intangible

Entrepreneur

Demand

Commercialisation

Adaptation

Risk

Capital

Market Research

Income

Revenue

The purpose of business activity

Write and illustrate some examples of goods and services in the table

Goods	Services

Many businesses exist so that they meet a certain need or fill a gap in the market. An entrepreneur may start an enterprise if there is a demand they can meet. This means thy have spotted an opportunity to meet needs, that no one else is meeting.

Business ideas can come about either as an original idea or an adaptation of an existing product or service. Explain the following and give real life examples:

Original Ideas	Adaptation
Invention	Innovation	

Businesses exist to meet what customers needs and wants. Define and give examples of both below.

Wants	Needs

Characteristics of an entrepreneur

In order to produce goods or services, businesses need to organise resources and consider how much risk they are willing to take. An entrepreneur will do this by considering resources available to them. Explain these and give examples of a consideration in the table below.

Land	Labour

Capital	Enterprise

For an entrepreneur to be successful at combining these, they need to have certain personal characteristics. These might include... (explain each in the table)

Creativity	Determination

Risk taking	Confidence

The concept of risk and reward

Business activity can pose different types of risk to the entrepreneur. Explain each o these types of risk:

Financial Loss	Lack of Security	Business Failure

Fill in the gaps

It is very difficult for an _____ to avoid risk, however by carrying out _____ _____ to find out what customers want, or by writing a _____ _____ to identify potential problems and ensuring that there is sufficient _____ available, and entrepreneur can minimise the _____.

There are also rewards for the entrepreneur for running a successful business: (complete the table)

Profit	Business Success	Independence

Knowledge Check

1. What is an example of a good?
2. What is a possible risk for someone starting their business?
3. What is an example of a want?
4. What is a need?
5. What is an example of innovation?
6. What is the purpose of business activity?
7. What is an invention?
8. What is an example of a service?
9. What is a reward for a successful business?
10. What are the 3 types of resource an entrepreneur must organise?

1.2 Business Planning

Define the key words

Aims and objectives

SMART

Target market

Revenue forecast

Cash flow forecast

Sources of finance

Marketing mix

Investors

Mortgage

The role ad importance of a business plan

A business plan is a document created by an entrepreneur that provides the details of all elements of the business. By creating one, it can support the entrepreneur with considering all elements of their business. Complete the table below explaining what sort of information would be found in each section:

Business idea	
Aims and objectives	
Target market	
Revenue forecast	
Projected costs and profit	
Cash flow forecast	
Sources of finance	
Location	
Marketing mix	

The purpose of planning business activity

Fill in the gaps

When an entrepreneur creates a _____ _____ they must consider all the key _____ and address any issues. They should complete market _____ to gain a good understanding of the market and where to _____ the business. Market research will also help them with creating the _____ and _____. There is 2 types of market research. Complete the table below explaining both types with examples

Primary research	Secondary research

The cash _____ forecast will also help to minimise _____. This is a prediction of what money a business may have over a set period of time. By completing the _____ _____ _____, the entrepreneur can see if there have been any changes/ times of year when they do not make _____.

Explain how a business plan can be used to obtain finance.

Knowledge Check

1. What is the first section in a business plan?
2. Name 3 other elements included in the business plan.
3. Name one stakeholder who might be interested in seeing a business plan.
4. What acronym is used to create business objectives?
5. How can a business plan be used to minimise risk?
6. What are the four elements of the marketing mix?
7. Why would a bank be interested in seeing a business plan?
8. Who else would be interested in seeing the business plan?
9. Name 2 types of forecast on the business plan.
10. What two categories of research might a business undertake in order t complete a business plan?

1.3 Business Ownership

Define the key terms

Debt

Creditor

Private limited company

Liability

Income tax

Share capital

Economies of scale

Hostile takeover

Companies House

Share holder

Share

Liability

Explain what each of these are, their potential implications, and the advantages and disadvantages of each.

Limited Liability	Unlimited Liability

Sole Trader

Characteristics	
Advantages	Disadvantages

Partnership

Some partnerships have limited liability and are know as limited liability partnerships (LLPs). They are covered by the limited liability partnerships Act 2000.

Characteristics	
Advantages	Disadvantages

Private Limited Company (Ltd)

Characteristics	
Advantages	Disadvantages

Public Limited Company (PLC)

Characteristics	
Advantages	Disadvantages

Knowledge Check

1. What type of liability does a sole trader have?
2. What is a private limited company abbreviated as?
3. What is a type of business that can sell shares to the general public?
4. State one thing true of a partnership that is not the case for a Ltd.
5. What does PLC stand for?
6. What is a benefit of being a in a partnership?
7. What is a disadvantage of being a sole trader?
8. What are the owners of a private or public limited company referred to as?
9. What does LLP stand for?
10. What is an advantage of being a sole trader?

1.4 Business aims and objectives

Define the key terms

Aims

Objectives

SMART objectives

Market Share

Survival

Aims and objectives

Business objectives are often created using the SMART acronym:

S

M

A

R

T

Businesses have two types of aims and objectives _____ and _____. Financial aims are linked to _____. Their goal is to make sure a business can afford to keep running or help it make a _____. An entrepreneur may have more than one financial _____ that they use to give their business direction

Complete the table below with detailed definitions and explanations

Business Survival	
Profit	
Sales	
Market Share	
Financial Security	

Non-financial aims and _____ are linked to anything other than making _____ for the business. These are usually linked to _____ reasons behind an entrepreneur setting up a business.

Complete the table below with detailed definitions and explanations

Social objectives	
Personal satisfaction	
Challenge	
Control	
Independence	

Knowledge Check

1. What is the difference between an aim and an objective?
2. What are two main types of objectives?
3. What are two main reasons why different businesses will have different aims and objectives?
4. Write a SMART target for a new business in their first year.
5. What is the difference between financial and non-financial objectives?
6. Write an example financial objective for a small business in their first year,
7. What does business survival mean?
8. What are the 5 types of non-financial objective?
9. What does profit mean?
10. Write an example of a non-financial objective for a small business in their first year.

1.5 Stakeholders in business

Key Words

Internal stakeholders

External stakeholders

Conflict

Pressure Groups

Dividends

Job security

Negotiation

Compromise

Business stakeholders

Internal stakeholders work within a business, external stakeholders are affected by the business activities and do not work for the company.

Define each of the 8 main types of stakeholder, and state whether they are internal or external.

Stakeholder	Internal or External	Definition
Shareholders & owners		
Managers		
Employees		
Customers		
Suppliers		
Local community		
Pressure groups		
Government		

Stakeholders objectives and impact

Complete the table giving examples of the priorities of each stakeholder and how they are affected by business activity.

Stakeholder	Priorities	How affected
Shareholders & owners		
Managers		
Employees		
Customers		
Suppliers		
Local community		
Pressure groups		
Government		

Stakeholders impact and conflicts

Complete the table giving examples of the stakeholder affects business activity and example of a possible conflict with another stakeholder.

Stakeholder	Impact	Conflict
Shareholders & owners		
Managers		
Employees		
Customers		
Suppliers		
Local community		
Pressure groups		
Government		

Knowledge Check

1. Give an example of internal stakeholders of a football club?
2. A business announces redundancies. Which stakeholder would not be affected by this?
3. What is a stakeholder?
4. What is an external stakeholder?
5. What stakeholder group is made up of people and organisations near to a business?
6. Which stakeholder usually has the most influence on business decisions?
7. What is a likely stakeholder objective of the government?
8. The owners of a business want to cut costs by using cheaper raw materials. Who could this cause a conflict with?
9. A business that offers good career progression is most likely to please which stakeholder group?
10. A business id found to be polluting a local water source. Which two stakeholders will this cause conflict between?

1.6 Business growth

Key words

Innovation

Inorganic Growth

Merger

Organic Growth

Research and Development

Takeover

Diversification

Internal growth

Fill in the Gap

Business growth is an important objective and may help to:

*

*

*

*

It can occur in several ways:

*

*

*

*

Internal growth can occur when a business chooses to expand through activities by either launching new products or by entering new markets

Explain how new products help a business to grow, you should include an example.

New Products

Businesses may enter new markets in order to achieve growth. Explain why entering a new market is more risky than introducing new products.

State and explain how a business can enter new markets in one of three ways:

*

*

*

Explain the advantages and disadvantages of internal growth

Advantages	Disadvantages

External growth

External growth usually involves a merger or takeover.

State and explain an example of a merger

State and explain an example of a takeover

There are 4 methods through which a business can merge with or take over another business, explain and illustrate.

Horizontal Integration	Forward Vertical Integration
Backward Vertical Integration	Conglomerate Integration

Explain the advantages and disadvantages of external growth

Advantages	Disadvantages

Fill in the gaps

When a business grows it may choose to become a public _____ company (PLC). In a PLC, the shares are sold to the _____ on the _____ market. People who own shares are called _____. The become part _____ of the business. When a business sells shares on the stock market this is known as _____ on the stock _____.

Explain the advantages and disadvantages of being a PLC

Advantages	Disadvantages

Capital found from within a business is an internal source of finance, and capital from outside of the business is an external source of finance.

Define and explain the source of finance and state its advantages and disadvantages

Internal

Retained Profits	
Advantages	Disadvantages

Selling of Assets	
Advantages	Disadvantages

The Owners Savings	
Advantages	Disadvantages

External

Loan Capital	
Advantages	Disadvantages

Share Capital	
Advantages	Disadvantages

Stock Market Floatation	
Advantages	Disadvantages

Knowledge check

1. What is one benefit of inorganic growth?
2. Define takeover.
3. What type of growth is hiring more staff an example of?
4. What is a disadvantage of organic growth?
5. What do economies of scale result in?
6. State one thing a PLC can do that a LTD cannot.
7. What type of growth would lead to a reduced number of businesses operating in the domestic market?
8. What is a benefit of using retained profit as a source of finance?
9. What method of growth is using e-commerce to sell goods an example of?
10. State one example of an internal source of finance.

2 Marketing

2.1 The role of marketing

Key terms

Price

Quality

Choice

Convenience

Identifying customers

Understanding customers

Customer wants and needs

Fill in the gaps

In order for an _____ to be successful, it is important that they are able to identify and meet customer _____. Most business ideas come from an entrepreneur spotting a need for a _____ or _____. There are _____ main areas of customer needs that an entrepreneur or small business must consider. These are p_____, q_____, c_____ and c_____.

Explain the following in terms of how they can be used to meet customer needs.

Price	
Quality	
Choice	
Convenience	

It is important for a business to identify who its customers or potential customers are and understand what they want. Identifying, understanding and meeting the requirements of customers means a new business can go two things: generate sales and survive.

Explain how the following can be influenced by a business being able to identify customers and their needs.

Generating Sales	
Business Survival	

Knowledge Check

1. What are the four customer needs?
2. What does business survival mean?
3. Why is choice and benefit for a business?
4. What does convenience mean?
5. What strategies could help a business generate more sales?
6. What is most important about the quality o a product or service?
7. What could an example of convenience be?
8. What could be a consequence of not charging an appropriate price for a product or service?
9. How would generating more sales help a business?

2.2 Market research

Key words

Focus group

Primary research

Qualitative data

Quantitative data

Secondary research

Market Research

When businesses are deciding how to develop their products and services, they undertake market research. Market research can either be done by the company itself or taken from elsewhere. Market research collects information that might help a business to be more successful and spot gaps in the market.

Fill in the gaps

One of the aims of market research is to _____ and understand the needs of _____ relating to price, _____, _____ and convenience. A business must make sure it is providing the right _____, at the right _____, in the right place, at the right time. By identifying the needs of customers through _____ research, businesses are able to _____ their level of risk and make business _____ that are more likely to be successful. Customer needs change over _____, so it is important for a business to keep up to date and be _____ with its products.

Another purpose of market research is to help a business identify _____ in the _____. This is an area where there is a demand for a product or service that is _____ being met. Spotting a gap in the market gives a new _____ a good chance of _____ as there will be _____ competition to begin with.

Market research is conducted to reduce risk and allow businesses to make better decisions.

State 5 ways a business can reduce risk through the use of market research

*

*

*

*

*

Market research can also help businesses make better decisions.

Write down an example of a business using market research to inform them with making better decisions.

Primary research is market research conducted by the business, and is bespoke to them and the information they gather.

Explain the examples of primary market research and complete the advantages and disadvantages of each.

Surveys	
+	-

Questionnaires	
+	-

Focus Groups	
+	-

Observations

+	-

Secondary research, also known as desk research, involves gathering data that already exists, both internally and externally to the business.

Internet research

+	-

Market reports

+	-

Government Reports

+	-

Explain the following include examples in your explanations.

Qualitative data	Quantitative data

Market research can also be gathered using social media, identify some advantages and disadvantages of using this method.

Advantages	Disadvantages
*	*
*	*
*	*
*	*

Knowledge Check

1. What is the purpose of market research?
2. Why is it important for a business to identify customer needs?
3. What is a gap in the market?
4. What are two main methods of market research?
5. Explain what a focus group is?
6. What is an advantage of secondary research?
7. What is a key characteristic of quantitative data?
8. What is one way a business could conduct external research?
9. What is one of the main pitfalls of using social media for market research?
10. Why is having market research data important?

2.3 Market Segmentation

Key words

Demographics

Lifestyle

Location

Market Segments

The Competition

Gap in the Market

Market Map

Market Segmentation

Fill in the gaps

Segmentation is how a business splits up its _____ market and is based on location, _____, behaviour, lifestyle, income and _____.

Complete the table, define and give an example of each

Location	
Demographics	
Behaviour	
Lifestyle	
Income	
Age	

Fill in the gaps

Market _____ is the process of using a _____ to plot competitors and their product to understand _____ behaviour and spot a _____ in the _____. It also allows a business to see who their _____ will be and what other products and _____ are available in the same sector. A market map is displayed as a graph and makes it very easy to see where gaps in the market exist. An entrepreneur can use a gap in the market to help them _____ a product or service that is more likely to be a _____.

Draw your own market map for different makes of car

Two elements that are commonly measured on a market map are q_____ and p_____.
Can you think of some other things which could be used the measure on a market map.

*

*

*

*

*

Knowledge Check

1. What does geographical segmentation refer to?
2. What does demographic segmentation relate to?
3. What is the purpose of a market map?
4. What two elements are commonly measured on a market map?
5. What is a gap in the market?
6. Give an example of using age as a method of market segmentation?
7. Purchasing behaviour at different times of the year and in different situations related to what kind of segmentation?

2.4 The marketing mix

Key Words

Price

Place

Product

Promotion

Aesthetics

Economic Manufacture

Extension Strategy

Function

Product Differentiation

Product Life Cycle

Profit Margins

Niche

Branding

E-Newsletters

Promotional Strategies

Sponsorship

Viral Advertising

Distribution

E-tailer

Retailer

Introduction to the marketing mix

Explain how a business should consider each of these in its marketing plan

Price	Place

Product	Promotion

The term competitive environment refers to the _____ placed on a business by its _____. Businesses that operate in a _____ market have a tough competitive environment as there are many other businesses offering very similar _____ or _____. This means that if a business charges too much then its customers will go _____. Business adapt their marketing _____ to try to convince customers that their product is better than the products of their _____. The aim of these adaptations is to gain _____ _____.

They can do this by:

*

*

*

*

Consumer needs can change over time one common trend is convenience. Businesses have had to alter their marketing mix by developing or adapting new or existing products to meet the customer needs.

Some ways businesses adapt to changing consumer needs are:

*

*

*

*

Explain the potential impact of technology on the marketing mix

*

*

*

Explain how e-commerce and digital communication can impact the marketing mix

*

*

*

*

Product

The three design factors _____, _____, and _____ are mixed together in different ways in order to appeal to different _____ markets.

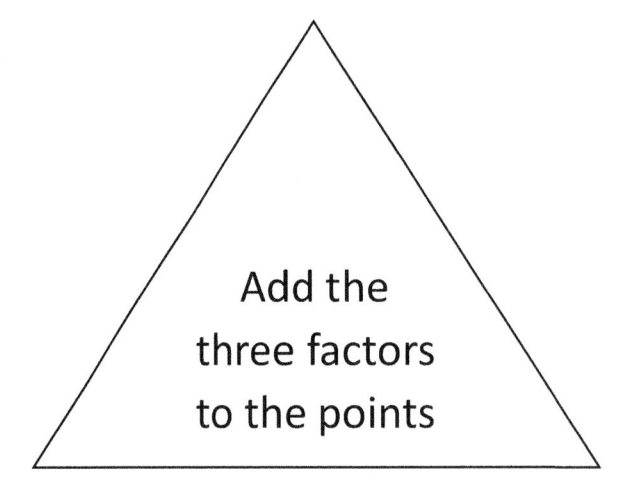

Add the three factors to the points

There are 4 phases of the product lifecycle. Explain each of the phases.

I_____	
G_____	
M_____	
D_____	

Complete and label the graph below to indicate the level of sales in each of the phases in the product life cycle.

How long a product lasts will depend on:

*

*

Extension strategies can be used to extend the life of a product. Mark and label on the diagram above where extension strategies would be used.

Explain the following 5 extension strategies.

Product Differentiation	
Reducing the price of the product	
Rebranding the product	
Repositioning the product	
Increasing marketing activity	

Price

The price of a product is how much a customer is asked to pay for an item. Businesses must consider several factors when setting prices. Complete the table explaining each factor.

The cost of making the product	
The quality of the product	
The brand image of the product	
The demand and supply of a product	

Business should choose between 2 methods of pricing. Explain both methods with an example and explain the advantages and disadvantages of each:

Pricing Low	
Advantages	Disadvantages

Pricing High	
Advantages	Disadvantages

Constantly changing markets mean that businesses will need to review their prices that they have set for their products on a regular basis. They must therefore look at factors that influence pricing strategies.

Complete the table explaining how each of these factors may influence the pricing strategy of the business.

Changes in Technology	
Number of Competitors	
Market Segments	
Where a Product is in its Life Cycle	

Promotion

There are 3 main purposes of promotion:

*

*

*

There are a range of methods a business can use. Explain each of these and use examples:

Sponsorship
Advertising
Product Trials
Special Offers
Branding

What is the effect of a good promotional strategy?

What is the effect of a poor promotional strategy?

Technology can be used by a business to aid promotion. Complete the table explaining each tool, and examples of how a business could use it.

Viral Marketing on Social Media
Targeted Online Advertising
Apps
E-Newsletters

Place

Fill in the gaps

Place is how goods and _____ reach customers. This includes how customers access products, and how products are _____ from producers to _____. The different ways of moving goods from producers to customers are called _____ of _____. These include _____, _____, and _____.

Explain the following and give examples.

Direct Channels of Distribution

Indirect Channels of Distribution

It is important to be able to recognise the difference between retailers, e-tailers and e-commerce. Explain the following, giving examples, and explaining the advantages and disadvantages of each.

Retailers	
Advantages	Disadvantages

E-tailers	
Advantages	Disadvantages

E-commerce	
Advantages	Disadvantages

The 4P's working together

Consider each element of the marketing mix and how a business needs consistency. Complete the table below

	Price	Place	Product	Promotion
How it influences price				
How it influences place				
How it influences product				
How it influences promotion				

The marketing mix can be used to gain a competitive advantage by offering products at lower prices or by adding value. If a business cannot lower the price of a product it is important to use the marketing mix to make it stand out. Complete the table below explaining how the marketing mix can do this.

Price	
Place	
Product	
Promotion	

A business can influence the competitive advantage it has over other businesses by creating a coherent and integrated marketing mix. A games console company introduces a new console, explain how they might build the marketing mix in the table below, you should include how these give it a competitive advantage.

Price	
Place	
Product	
Promotion	

Knowledge Check

1. Give an example of a product with a USP.
2. Define the marketing mix.
3. A retailer is offering 15% off the usual price of a product. What element of the marketing mix is influencing price?
4. A trainer company introduces anti-stink shoes. What element of the marketing mix is it using to gain a competitive advantage?
5. What is the main purpose of marketing?
6. Define special offer.
7. Define targeted online marketing.
8. What is an example of using brand identity for product promotion?
9. What enables some manufacturers to charge higher prices to their competitors' identical products?
10. If a product sells out fast and the retailer increases the price. What factors has the retailer considered in its pricing decision?

3 People

3.1 The role of human resources

Key words

Human resources

Induction

Legislation

The role of Human resources

Businesses need to carry out their day to day activities, human resources is the coordination of all business activity which related to employees, which are needed for business activity. Mind map below all the activities human resources are responsible for:

To meet the needs of the business, human resources must work with other departments, and must consider the following. Explain the importance of each of these.

The number of staff needed	The staffing budget
The types of contract staff will be offered	The location of staff
How staff will be managed	How legislation will be met

Knowledge Check

Answer the following in detail

1. Outline the importance of a human resource department in business activity.
2. Explain the impact of an ineffective human resource department.

3.2 Organisational structures and different ways of working

Key Words

Centralised organisations

Decentralised organisations

Flat Structure

Hierarchical structure

Organisational chart

Flexible hours

Freelance contract

Permanent contract

Remote working

Temporary Contract

Communication

Barrier to communication

Insufficient communication

Excessive communication

Organisational structure

An organisation can use a tall or flat structure. Draw a diagram to represent each type

Hierarchical Structure	Flat Structure

There are a number of key terms we can apply to organisational structures, define each of these:

Span of control

Chain of command

Delayering

Delegation

Subordinates

There are two main forms of organisational structures:

Centralised management structure	
Advantages	Disadvantages

Decentralised management structure	
Advantages	Disadvantages

Different ways of working

Employees usually work in one of 3 ways when they are employed. Explain each below and give examples.

Full time

Part time

Flexible hours and zero-hours contracts

When workers are given a job by a business, their work is agreed in one of three types of contract. Explain each type of contract giving an example of they type of job role suited to the contract.

Permanent

Temporary

Freelance

Technology has had a huge impact on how businesses operate and how employees work. Two main ways it has changed businesses is increasing efficiency and remote working. Explain both in the space provided.

Increased efficiency	Remote working

Communication

Communication is important in a business, when it is ineffective it can fall into 2 categories. Explain each and the negative impacts they can have.

Insufficient Communication

Excessive Communication

Some barriers to communication include:

*

*

*

*

*

*

*

Outline the impact on a business of poor communication.

Knowledge Check

1. What is an organisational structure?
2. What is a chain of command?
3. What does the term delayering mean?
4. What is a subordinate?
5. What type of organisational structure is a small business most likely to have?
6. What is a part time employee?
7. What happens in decentralised management?
8. Describe a permanent contract.
9. What does the term remote working refer to?
10. How could excessive communication impact a business?

3.3 Communication in business

Key words

Channel of communication

Internal communication

External communication

Video conference

Jargon

Ways of communicating

Fill in the gaps

Communication is the process of _____ and _____ information using a channel of _____. Internal communication occur within the business, external communication takes place between the business and other people from outside the company. Communication can be both _____ and _____.

Explain the following types of communication, you should explain whether they are internal or external, and whether they are formal or informal.

Letter	
Email	
Text Message	
Phone Call	
Meeting	
Presentation	
Video	
Social Media	
Website	

The importance of business communication

Outline the barriers to communication:

Poor explanations	
Poor spelling and grammar	
Incorrect language	
Technology issues	
Poor structuring of information	
Jargon, technical language or slang	
Lack of understanding	

Poor communication can have negative impacts, explain the consequences of the following

Mistakes

Confusion

Poor Reputation

Can you add any others?

The influence of digital communication on business activity

Common ways of communicating digitally include:

*

*

*

*

*

Outline how these have influenced business activity:

Improved speed and accuracy	Improved productivity
Better customer service	Access to a wider audience

Knowledge Check

1. What is an example of digital communication?
2. What is an example of internal communication?
3. What is the best way to share a formal report with a colleague?
4. What is an example of formal communication?
5. Define external communication?
6. What would you call information that is shared casually?
7. What can be a barrier to effective communication?
8. What is a disadvantage of digital communication?
9. What type of communication is a letter?
10. What is the result of poor communication?

3.4 Recruitment and selection

Key words

Application form

CV (Curriculum Vitae)

External recruitment

Internal recruitment

Job description

Person specification

References

Recruitment

Businesses employ staff to take on a number of different roles, which are then organised into a hierarchy. Outline the following roles:

Directors

Senior managers

Supervisors and team leaders

Operational staff

Support staff

Recruitment is the process of deciding who will fulfil a job role. There is a number of documents involved in the recruitment process. Explain who creates and what is included in the following documents.

Person specification	Application form
Job description	CV

Businesses recruit for new roles from both internal and external applicants. Complete the table explaining the advantages and disadvantages of each

Internal	External
Advantages	Advantages
Disadvantages	Disadvantages

Knowledge Check

1. What is the name for the group of people at the top of a business?
2. What is the role of operational staff in a business?
3. What does internal recruitment mean?
4. What information does a job description include?
5. What does the term recruitment mean?
6. What information does a CV include?
7. Where might a business advertise a job role externally?
8. What is the role of supervisors and team leaders in a business?
9. What is an advantage of internal recruitment?
10. What is an advantage of external recruitment?

3.5 Motivation and retention

Key words

Autonomy

Commission

Fringe benefits

Job enrichment

Job rotation

Remuneration

Motivation

Explain the following in terms of motivating employees.

Motivation	Attract employees
Retention	Productivity

Businesses can use financial methods to motivate their employees. Explain with examples the following examples.

Remuneration

Bonuses

Commission

Promotions

Fringe benefits

Non-financial methods of motivation include the following, explain with examples.

Job rotation

Job enrichment

Autonomy

Knowledge Check

1. What is motivation?
2. Why is retaining employees important to businesses?
3. How is productivity linked to motivation?
4. What s remuneration?
5. What is a bonus?
6. What is an example of a fringe benefit?
7. What is autonomy?
8. What is job rotation?
9. What is an example of job enrichment?
10. How might a promotion increase an employee's motivation?

3.6 Training and development

Key words

Formal training

Informal training

Mentor

Ongoing training

Performance reviews

Retention

Self-learning

Target-setting

Training

There are several types of training and development. Outline the examples stated below.

Formal training

Informal training

Self-learning

Ongoing training

Target Setting

Performance reviews (appraisals)

Businesses train and develop their employees for a number of reasons. Two main reasons are motivation and retention. Explain each below

Motivation	Retention

Technology becomes increasingly importance as it further advances. Explain the impact of new technology on effective training and development of staff.

Knowledge Check

1. What do the terms training and development refer to?
2. What is formal training?
3. What is formal training also referred to as?
4. What is an example of informal training?
5. What is a performance review also known as?
6. What is the purpose of performance reviews?
7. What does the term retention refer to?
8. What is motivation?
9. What is a benefit of training employees to use new technology?
10. What is a good retention rate?

3.7 Employment law

Key Words

Red tape

Legislation

Principes of employment Law

In the UK there are 4 areas of employment legislation that form the basis of employee rights in the workplace;

Recruitment	Pay
Discrimination	Health & Safety

Explain how legislation affects recruitment

While recruiting new staff (Equality Act, 2010; Data Protection Act, 2018)	Once new staff have been recruited (Employment Rights Act, 1996; Pensions Act, 2008)

In terms of legislation complete the following with regards to pay

What businesses must do (National Minimum Wage Act, 1998)	What businesses must not do (The Equality Act, 2010)

The Equality Act (2010) is designed to prevent discrimination. Complete the table with the protected characteristics and requirements of the Equality Act.

Characteristic	Requirements of Equality Act 2010
Age	
Disability	
Gender Reassignment	
Marital Status	

Pregnancy and Maternity	
Race	
Religion	
Sex	
Sexual Orientation	

The Health and Safety at Work Act (1974) outlines responsibilities that both employers and employees have.

Employers should provide:

*

*

*

*

*

Employees are expected to:

*

*

*

*

Working Time Regulations (1998, 2003) limits hours these are:

*

*

*

*

*

Costs of meeting legislation, complete the table below with examples of additional costs that could be incurred by employer by the legislation:

Act	Example of additional cost
Health and Safety at Work Act (1974)	
Employment Rights Act (1996)	
National Minimum Wage Act (1998)	
Working Time Regulations (1998, 2003)	
Pensions Act (2008)	

Equality Act (2010)	
Data Protection Act (2018)	

Consequences of meeting legal obligations	Consequences of not meeting legal obligations

Knowledge Check

1. Which act makes employers responsible for providing a safe working environment?
2. State one consequence of failing to comply with employment laws?
3. What act tackles discrimination?
4. Give an example of something employment law prevent businesses using to discriminate against staff?
5. Give an example of an increase in staff wage costs due to consumer legislation.
6. State a reason for a business to comply with consumer legislation.
7. What issues are covered by employment law?
8. Give an example of a situation where a business is not complying with employment law.

Printed in Great Britain
by Amazon